TARKASANGRAHA

(Basic Principal of Nyaya)

TARKASANGRAHA

(Basic Principal of Nyaya)

BY

ANNA BHATTA.

EDITED WITH AN ENGLISH TRANSLATION

BY

PANDIT JIBANANDA VIDYASAGARA B. A.

Published by

GYAN

Gyan Publishing House
5, Ansari Road
Daryaganj, New Delhi-110002
Phone: 011-47034999, 9811692060
E-mail: books@gyanbooks.com

Distribution Network
gyanbooks.com
India, USA, Canada, UK, Australia, France

ISBN : 978-81-212-2468-0 (PB)
First Published, 1872

2nd Impression 2021

Printed at: Gyan Press, Delhi.

Tarkasangraha
(Basic Principal of Nyaya)
Author: Anna Bhatta

TARKASANGRAHA

BY

ANNA BHATTA.

EDITED WITH AN ENGLISH TRANSLATION

BY

PANDIT JIBANANDA VIDYASAGARA B. A.

Calcutta:

PRINTED AT THE SARASUDHANIDHI PRESS.

1872.

To be had from Pandit Jibananda Vidyasagara B. A. Govt. Sanskrit College of Calcutta.

अवतरणिका ।

प्रणम्य परमात्मानं श्रीजीवानन्द शर्म्मणा ।

इंलण्डभाषया तर्कसंग्रहोऽयमनूद्यते ॥ १ ॥

प्रायो नृपप्रियतमेष्विह भाषितेषु

लोके समादृतिरतिप्रथिता समन्तात् ।

इंलण्डभाषितमतः सुमतं जनानां

तत्पाटवेन महिमानमुपैति लोकः ॥ २ ॥

तदादरेणापरभाषितेषु

श्रद्धा परं हीयत एव नृणाम् ।

तेषां प्रचारेण च सर्वदेशे

प्रायो विलुप्तेतरशास्त्रचर्चा ॥ ३ ॥

संस्कारयुक्तां विदुषां गिरं मनाक्

इंलण्डभाषासु कृतश्रमाणाम् ।

यथा प्रचार्य्येत सुतर्कविद्या

तथावबोधाय ममैष यत्नः ॥ ४ ॥

तेषां विबोधनकृते निजभाषयैव

डाक्तर्विलसिन्नविदा वितता पुरा या ।

रोयेरष्टाक्तरवरेण च भिन्नयाक्तै:
सवादनेन विदुषा विपुलोन्नता सा ॥ ५ ॥

तयो: काञ्चित् पङ्क्तिं क्वचिदपि च तत्तद्वचनतो
गृहीत्वा सारांशं स्वमतिमनुसृत्यापि च मया।
अनूद्यैषां ग्रन्थे विरचितमिदं लण्डनगिरा
हृदि स्थानं दत्त्वा सफलयतु विद्वान् श्रममिमम् ॥ ६ ॥

श्रीदामोदरगोविन्द-समाख्यस्य द्विजन्मन:।
प्रीत्यानुष्टेन च मया सन्दर्भोऽयं विनिर्म्मित: ॥ ७ ॥

यदि प्रमादोऽत्र ममास्ति कश्चित्
विद्वद्वरैरेष विमार्ज्जनीय:।
दोषानुसन्धानपरा न सन्तो
गुणैकपक्षा: प्रथिताहि लोके ॥ ८ ॥

येषां हितार्थाय कृता मयैषा
तेषां मुदे स्याद्यदि सा समर्था।
तदैव मे यत्नचय: फलप्रदो
न चान्यथेत्येव विचिन्तनीयम् ॥ ९ ॥

शाके वेदाङ्कबाहेन्दु-मिते शौरश्रुचौ मया।
निर्म्माय मुद्रिता यत्नात् तर्कसंग्रहदीपिका ॥ १० ॥

TRANSLATION

OF THE

TARKA SANGRAHA.

—oo—

1. "Having treasured in my mind the Lord of the universe, and having taken the dust of the feet of my preceptor, this collection of the Philosophical Discussions, is made by me, to make the subject easy to the understanding of those who are not well off in the subject."

2. "There are seven categories (*padarthas*);—I. Substance (*dravya*), II. Quality (*guna*), III. Action (*karma*), IV. Generality (*samanya*), V. Particularity (*vishesha*), VI. Intimate Relation (*samavaya*), VII. negation (*abhava*).

Padartha is not exactly what Aristotle meant by category; but as most of Aristotle's categories refer to classes of existence or to what is most nearly related to them, and as in modern philosophy the term category expresses almost universally this meaning, we may safely adopt it here, viz. as refering to the notions, which express the general forms of knowledge or what is the same, the general modes of existence.

There are different sets of Categories according to different schools of philosophy. Those of Aristotle are as follows :—

1. Substance. 2. Quantity. 3. Quality. 4. Relation 5. Place. 6. Time. 7. Condition. 8. Possession. 9. Action. 10. Passion.

Those of Zoroaster are as follows :—

I. Sensation. II. Intelligence. III. Judgment. IV. Conscience. V. Life.

Those of Locke are as follows :—

I. Extension. II. Solidity. III. Mobility. IV. Perceptibility. V. Motivity. VI. Perceptibility. VII. Motivity. VIII. Existence. IX. Duration. X. Number.

The number of seven catagories is adopted by the Veiseshikas, and also acknowledged by the followers of the Nyaya, as established in the Bhashya.

Kanada acknowledged only the six Categories, excluding negation. Gautama, the founder of the Nyaya, enumerates under the head of objects of proof (categories.)

1. Soul, 2. body, 3. sense, 4. object of sense, 5. intellect, 6. mind, 7. activity, 8. fault, 9. condition of the, soul after death (transmigration), 10, retribution, 11. pain 12. deleverance from pain.

The enumeration of the Subdivisions of Categories.

3. " The Substances are nine in number : 1. earth (*prithivi.*), 2. Water (*ab*), 3. light (*tejas*), 4. air (*vayu*), 5. ether (*akasa*), 6. time (*kala*), 7. space (*dik*), 8. soul (*atman*), 9. mind (*manas*)."

Time and space are here classed as substances, because the word substance is employed to signify that to which qualities can be attributed. To explain this more fully, it is the substratum of qualities either in the relation of intimate union (samavaya sambandha) or in the relation af antecedent negation (pragabhava) that is of future existance.

4. "The qualities are twenty-four in number,)

1. Color (*rupa*), 2. taste (*rasa*), 3. smell (*gandha*), 4. touch (*sparsa*), 5. number (*sankhya*), 6. quantity (*parimana*), 7. individuality (*prithaktwa*), 8. conjunction (*sanyoga*), 9. disjunction (*vibhaga*), 10. priority (*paratwa*), 11. posteriority (*aparatwa*), 12. gravity (*gurutwa*), fluidity (*dravatwa*), 14. viscidity (*sneha*), 15 sound (*sabda*), 16. intellect (*buddhi*), 17. pleasure (*Sukha*), 18. pain (*dukha*), 10 desire (*ichhha*), 20. aversion (*dwesha*), 21. volition (prayatna), 22. virtue, (*dharma*), 23. vice (*adharma*), 24. faculty (*sanskara*).

5. " There are five actions.

1. Throwing upwards (*utkshepana*), 2. throwing downwards (*abakshepana*), 3. contracting (*akunchana*) 4. expanding (*prasarana*), 5. going on (gamana)."

The last of these, *viz* gamana or " motion in general, inludes all sorts of motion not mentioned before.

6. " Generality is considered two fold, extensive (para) and non-extensive (apara)."

These correspond to genus and species. Existence, referring substances, qualities and actions is called extensive. The class which differs from this is called non-extensive; substantiality and similar notions are extensive and non-extensive. It is called extensive by its including many things; by its being included in a more extensive class it is non-extensive.

6, 'But the ultimate conditions of eternal Substances such as mind, Soul, time, place and the atoms of which the earth, water &c. are composed) are called particularities which are endless."

Such is the relation of a substance with its componing parts, as of a jar, &c. with its two halves, &c.; further the relation of substances with qualities and actions, and lastly the relation of substances, qualities and actions with their respective classes is called intimate relation. Intimate relation means constant relation.

7. " But the Intimate relation is of only one kind."

"Negation or non-existence (*abhaba*) is of four kinds;—antecedent negation (*pragabhava, or the state of a thing before it began to be*), destruction (*pradhansabhava*), absolute negation (*atyantabhava*), reciprocal negation (*anyonnyabhava.*)"

Negation is the reciprocal negation of the six categories, that is to say negation arises from the six categories being denied of each other. Negation is two-fold, universal negation and mutual negation. Universal negation is negation, different from mutual negation. Mutual negation is the negation of identity. Universal negation is of three kinds, antecedent, emergent, and absolute negation. In this half, a jar is to be produced; in this half a jar is to be destroyed; there is no jar; these are respectively the three negations, mentioned above.

Having thus classified the categories, the author proceeds to consider in detail each of the subdivisions.

8. " Earth has the peculiar quality of smell. It is of two kinds—eternal and non-eternal. It is eternal in the form of atoms; non-eternal in the form of aggregates or products viz. if consisting of two three &c. atoms."

The non-eternity of earth in the form of products indicates the want of permanence in the forms, such as jars, &c, which it may take. The jar, when broken to pieces as atoms, is no longer a jar, but the earth, of which it is composed, still remains. The existence of eternal atoms has been a favorite theory of several schools of philosophy. Among the Greeks, Epicurus is one of the most renowned of the maintainers of the atomic theory. The doctrine has been resumed by some modern chemists, not as an established fact but as a hypothesis which supplies terms very advantageous in enunciating the chemical laws of Definite Proportions.

"It (*earth composed of parts*) again is of three kinds, through the division of organized body (*sarira* organ of sense (*indriga*), object or inorganic matter (*vishaya*). We the mortals possess the organized body of the earth; the smell is the organ of sense of the earth, which receives odour, residing in the fore part of the nose; the inorganic matter of the earth is clay, stone and the like."

9. "Water is cool to the feel. And this (*water* is of two kinds—eternal and non-eternal, eternal, in the shape of atoms and non-eternal in the shape of products from the by-atomical to the highest compound.

"These compounds are again of three kinds;—the organized body; the organ of sense, and the inorganic matter.

Its organized body is to be met with in the realms of Varuna (*or Neptune*); its organ of sense is tongue (*rasana*) which relishes taste, residing in the forepart of the tongue; its inorganic matters or objects (*visayas*) are rivers, seas, &c."

10. "Light is hot to the feel. It is of two sorts—eternal in the form of atoms and non-eternal or transient in the form of compounds. These products or compounds are again of three kinds:—the organized body, the organ of sense and the inorganic

matter. It is well known that the organized body of light abides in the solar realm; the organ of sense of light is sight (*chakhas*) the recipient of colour, residing in the forepart of the black pupil of the eye; inorganic light is of four sorts, according to the division of earthy (*bhauma*), celestial (*divya*), intestinal (*audarya*) and mineral (*akaryja*). Earthy light, is that of fire, &c. celestial light is such as lightening &c. is without fuel. Intestinal is the cause of the digestion of what is eaten and drunk. Mineral light is found in mines, as gold, &c."

The Nyaya philosophy considers light and heat as one and the same thing. Modern chemists have found out curious resemblances not only between light and heat but also between these and electricity and magnetism; but whether they are materially the same or different has not yet been ascertained by experiment and examination. In the Nyaya the organ of seeing is supposed to be a ray of light emitted forth by the centre of the eye towards the external object that is seen. The Buddhists suppose that the organ of seeing is the pupil of the eye itself. The optists of the present day affirm that we see an object not because a ray emanates from the pupil of the eye towards the object viewed and ellumines it, but because the object reflects light on the retina of the eye.

The theory of the intestinal heat appears to be a prediction of Leibig's doctrine of digestion which ascribes to the body the function of a furnace having the food as fuel.

As the strongest heat of a furnace is unequal to calcine gold or turn it into an earthly looking oxide, it is supposed by the Naiyayikas as a lucid substance and not an earthly matter like the other metals.

In the Mimansa, gold is considered as a different substance altogether. This theory is adopted by the modern chemists of Europe.

11. "The feel in the air is considered peculiar to itself. The air is also supposed to have no colour. It is of two kinds, eternal and non-eternal :—eternal in the form of atoms—and non-eternal in the form of compounds or products. These compounds again are of three kind :—I. The organized dody; II. the organ of sense and III. the inorganic matter. The organized bodies of air are in the aerial region (evil spirits, such as the pisachas); its organ of sense the percipient of touch, is the skin (twak) which extends over the whole body. Its inorganic matters are those which cause the trembling of the trees and the like."

12. "The air that circulates within the body is called the vital air (*prana*) and this, though single, receives the defferent denomiminations of breathing, flatulence &c. through the distinction of modifying circumstances.

13. "The distinguishing quality of the ether is sound. It ts one, all pervading, and eternal. Time (*kala*),though one is the cause of the employment of the terms past and the like. It is all pervading and eternal."

The element of ether is inferred in order to account ior sound. As pure air and water are destitute of smell, ft has been concluded by the Naiyayikas that the smell is the distinctive proof of earth :—the perception of savour depending on the presenee of moisture in the mouth, it was concluded that the sense of taste must be aqueous in its nature :—the relation between light and vision was plain enough :—and the air having been appropriated to the sense of touch, which surrounds the whole body just as the air usually surrouuds it, there remains nothing else to support the uniformity of the system than to infer a fifth ' elementary essence for the substratum of sound which elementary essence is designated as ether. A fifth element, under the denomination of Quintissence,. was acknowledged by the antient philosophers of Europe, though with a different signification from that of the Nyaya system.

The doctrine that the organs of sense must resemble in their nature the objects which they were to apprehend is equivalent to the doctrine of a long predominance in Europe :—"that a cause must resemble its effect." It is in some points, the converse of the theory of ideas or sensible forms. In that theory outward bodies were supposed to emit forth refined images of themselves to the mind through the organs of sense. Here, on the other hand, the mind is supposed to send forth an organ of sense towards its object in the external world, resembling the object itself.

Thus bright bodies are represented as being viewed by means of a ray of light that emanates from the eye, and which constitutes the sense of sight.

Time, the producer of all productions, is the substrate of the world. This is proved by the perception of the " now ". If for instance the perception : " here is now a jar, " is given there exists a union between the motion of the sun and the jar. This is not conjunction or any other relation (for conjunction is between the parts of two or more things,) but it is a relation *of a different kind,* which is produced by time. That time is to be thought under the notion of a substratum, is evident from its being the cause of priority and posteriority. Time is the special (non-general) cause of the perception f priority and posteriority. Or if both definitions are combined. Time is the substrate of the special union, which is the non-intimate cause of priority and posteriority.

Although one, it has many names, viz moment, hour day &c., past, future and present time. Past is the time, whose destruction is the present, as yesterday; future is the time, whose future existence is present, as to-morrow, and present is the time, whose future existence is destroyed and whose destruction is (to come to pass) future, as to-day. There will, after every future moment, be another moment, because there will be always another action (the junction of which with other things produces the relation of time); this will be cause at the general conflagration, where also the terms of "moment," "day," &c. are applied.

14. "Space (*dik*) is the cause of the use of the terms *eastern* and the like. It is one, eternal, and all-pevading (*or infinite.*)"

15. "The repository of knowledge is the Soul (*atman*). It is of two kinds—the human Soul, and the divine Soul. The divine Soul is God who is Omniscient and one only—devoid of happiness and misery. The human Soul is different in each human body and is infinite and eternal."

The reason ascribed for the theory that the human soul is infinite is this, that, wherever the body goes, there the soul too is present. The human soul is the intimate cause of happiness and unhappiness &c., and the substantiality of it is proved by its being the substratum of the qualities: happiness and unhappiness. Since such causes as merit and demerit do not exist with regard to God or the devine Soul, he is not subject to either happiness and unhappiness.

The human Soul governs the organs of sense, &c because it successively, produces the conscience of the senses and of the body. Although there is in the soul the perception: I know, I am happy, &c., yet it cannot at first be proved against one who holds the contrary opinion, that the soul is something different from the body, &c. To prove this, it is said that "an instrument must possess its agent." As an instrument, has no effect without an agent, so also the eye and the other senses, which are the instruments for knowledge, have no effect without an agent. For this reason an independent agent is assumed.

To show, that the body is not the agent, it is urged that "there is no consciousness in the body, as is proved by the disappearance of consciousness after death," and also "if consciousness belonged to the body, there could in old age be no recollection of things, perceived in childhood, the body being subject to increase and decrease by acquiring and losing its particles," consciousness can neither belong to the senses; for if such were the case, how could recollection remain, when the senses are destroyed?

Let then consciousness not belong to the senses (external) but be maintained for the eternal mind To which the answer is :—the mind cannot be the Site of consciousness ;—for then knowledge and other internal qualities would remain imperceptible. Because as the mind is an atom, and as the cause of every perception is a certain greatness, no perception could take place, if knowledge, happiness, &c. were placed in the eternal mind. How mind is an atom, is explained afterwards. Consciousness then must belong to the soul.

Having finished the account of substance, the author goes on to treat of quality.

16. "Mind (*manas*) is that organ of sense which is instrumental to the apprehension of happiness and misery &c. It is endless, as each soul possesses one mind. It is in the form of an atom and is eternal."

The *Naiyayikas* are of opinion that the mind is small, as an atom, because if it were infinite, as the *Mimańsakas* uphold, it might be in union with all substances simultaneouly, and all sensations might be contemporaneous. Various sensations, the *Naiyayikas* maintain, do not arise at once to the same soul. They only appear to do so when passing in rapid succession; as a firebrand, whirled with velocity, looks like a ring of fire.

Of Qualities.

17. "The quality, that is apprehended by the eye only, is colour. Through the division of white, blue yellow, red, green, orange, and variegated, it is of seven kinds. All these seven colours are to be found in earth. The colour that is to be found in water is non-resplendant white. In light it is to be found both white and bright."

The great Newtom has discovered that the colour is in light only, and that a ray of light can be analysed into all the seven primary colours by means of a glass-prism. He has also proved by experiment that the variety of colours that is visible in the universe is owing to the variety of powers which different objects possess to absorb some primary colours and to emit forth the residue of the ray.

18. "The quality that is apprehended by the ongue is taste. And that is of six kinds through

the division of sweet, acid, saline, bitter, astringent, and pungent. All these six qualities of taste can be had in earth but in water the sweet taste can only be found."

19. "The quality that is apprehended by the nose is smell. And it is of two kinds, fragrance and non-fragrance which exist in earth only."

(20) "The quality that is apprehensive only by the organ of touch is feel. It is three-fold, cold, hot, and temperate (ie neither cold nor hot). It exists in earth, water, light, and air. The feel that is in water is cold, the feel that is in light is hot, and the feel that is in both the earth and air is neither cold nor hot."

Feel is perceived by the skin, it is the cause of perception through the skin. It is three-fold, tepid, cold, and warm. Hardness and similar qualities are in the earth. It is eternal in the atoms of water, light, and air, non-eternal in the atoms of earth.

The qualities of colour, taste, smell, and feel, as abiding in earth, they are produced by a cause, because by the union with fire, the colour, taste, and smell and feel of earth are changed ; not so as abiding in water, &c. be a hundred times boiled, yet no change of its colour, &c. takes place. The smell and heat of water, *on the other hand*, are artificial, because they are present or absent by the presence or absence of artificial means, like the cold feel of air and earth.

The *Vaiseshikas* affirm, that as to earth the change by the process of cooking takes place in the atoms. Their view is, as follows:—as long as the parts are retained in the compound, no change by the process of cooking is possible ; but when by the union of fire the compound substances have been destroyed, that change takes place in the atoms whic h have beccme independent of ea other. And again by the union of the atoms which, have been changed by the process of cooking, a production is effected from the compound of two, three, &c. atoms again to a componnd of many parts; for by the extraordinary velocity of heat the transition from the destruction of one compound to the production of another is sudden. Then from the destruction of a compound of two atoms, by a new production, a compound possessed of shape, &c., is formed in a few moments.

The Naiyayikas on the other hand affirm, that in compounds also, viz, in compounds of two, three &c., atoms, change by the process of cooking takes place. Their opinion is as follows:—The compound substances have pores, the minute parts of fire enter into the inside, and therefore change by the process of cooking is possible although the parts be retained in the compound.

(21) "The four qualities, colour &c., which are produced by the application of heat, are transient; but when they are not produced by the application of heat, they are either eternal or non-eternal or transient:—they are eternal in the eternal matters (atoms) and non-eternal or transient in the non-eternal or transient matters (objects produced, such as compounds."

(22)" The non-general or special cause of the application of the terms one, &c., is Number. It pervades all the nine substances. Beginning from one, it reaches to the highest numerical figure (pararddha.) Unity is either eternal or non-eternal; eternal when apertains to objects eternal, and non-eternal or transient when apertains to objects non-eternal or transient. But duality, &c., are every where non eternal or transient."

The highest numerical figure "parardha" is "many lacks of karors." The transient unity means this:—that when an object is broken into two pieces, it leaves on the moment, its character of unity and assumes the character of duality.

(23) "The non-general or special cause of the use of measure, is Quantity. It abides in all the nine substances; and it is of four kinds, minute and great, longe and short."

(24) "The non-general or special cause of the application of the term *separate*, is Individulity, which quality abides in all the substances."

(25) "The special or non-general cause of the use of the term "connected," is conjunction. It pervades all the substances."

(26) "Disjunction is that quality which causes the destruction of conjunction. All the substances are ts site."

"Distance and proximity or priority and posteriority are the two special or non-general causes of the application of the terms *far* and *near*, *ancient* and *recent*. Having been incident to four substances beginning with the earth and to the mind, they are of two kinds what is made by *space* and what is made by *time* With reference to an object placed far off, there is the *distance* made by *space*. With reference to an object placed near, there is *proximity* made by *space*. When an object is old there is *priority* with reference to *time.* When an object is *young,* there is *posteriority* with reference to *time.*"

(27) "The instrumental cause of a body's beginning to fall is *weight or gravity* which abides in earth and water."

(28) "The instumental cause of the first commencement of tickling is Fluidity which abides in earth, water and light. It is of two kinds:— natural (or primary) and adscititious (or secondary). It is natural (or primary, in water and adscititious (or secondary *i e* produced by somethiny else) in earth and light. In earthly substances such as clarified butter, &c,fluidity is caused by the application of heat".

(29) "The quality that causes infinitessimal particles to assume the shape of a mass is Viscidity: It exists in water alone".

The Naiyaikas maintain that oily Substances are viscid, only because they contain water. This phenomenon according to modern Chemists falls under the category of attraction of cohesion.

(30) "The quality that is apprended by the organ of hearing (*Sotra*) is sound (*Sabda*). It is two-fold, inarticulate and articulate. Inarticulate sound is that of a bugle, &c. Articulate Sound is in the form of the Sanscrit and other languages."

(31)"The quality that is the cause of the appliction of all terms is intellect or knowledge (*buddhi*). It is of two kinds, Memory and Apprehension. Knowledge (or a state of consciousness), which is caused by the internal reflexion of previous impressions (*Sanskara* is called memory (*smriti*). Knowledge different from that, is called apprehension (*anuvaba*). That is of two kinds, true apprehension and false apprehension.

(32) "Apprehension of an object in its real nature, is true apprehension. Thus the knowledge that 'it is silver' which we arrive at after, seeing true silver is called true apprehension. That is truly called the *prama* i e knowledge unmistakeable. False apprehension is that which indicates a nature that does not belong to the object of which the apprehension is formed. For instance, the apprehension 'This is silver' in a pearl-shell is a false apprehension."

(33) "True apprehension is of four kinds:—preceptions, inferences, comparisons and testimonies. Their causes are also four-fold, viz. perception inference, comparison, and testimony."

True apprehension is an apprehension without error. It is not perceived but by itself, by the concurrence of doubts. The *Mimansakas* say, that true apprehension is comprehended by itself. According to the *Gurus* a knowledge is a true aprehension by its own manifestation.

According to the opinion af the *Murarimisras* knowledge is obtained by reflection.

(34)" An efficient cause, that is not general to many effects, is called a special cause. That antecedent which invariably and unconditionally precedes an effect is called a *cause.* That is called an *effect,* of which, there was a previous non-existence."

(35) "Cause is three-fold, through the divisions of intimate, non-intimate, and instrumental. That from which in its intimate relation an effect is

produced is called an intimate cause, as threads are of cloth, and the cloth itself of its own colour, &c.

Where the cause and effect are associated in one and the same object, that cause is called non-intimate; such as the conjunction of the threads is the nonintimate cause of cloth, and the colour of the threads is that of the cloth itself; and the third, that is, the instrumental cause must be considered, what is different from either, such as the weaver's brush, the loom, &c., are of cloth. Among these three kinds of causes, that cause which is not general, is called the instrumental cause.'"

(36) "The instrumental cause of preception is sensation; sensation is the knowledge that is produced by the union of an organ of sense with an external object. This knowledge, which is called sensation, is two-fold; what admits of an alternative and what does not. The knowledge that admits of an alternative is indefinite, such as in the simple notion that "this is some-thing." The knowledge that does not admit of an alternatlve is definite such as, in the positive cognitions of 'this is Dittha' & 'This is a Brahman,' 'This is black.'

(37) "The Intercourse (*Sannikarsa*) of an organ of sense with anexternal object, which is the instrumental cause of preception, is of six kinds as follows:—

I. Conjunction, II. intimate union with that which is in conjunction, III. intimate union with what is intimately united with that which is in conjunction, IV. intimate union, V. intimate union with that which is intimately united, and VI. the union which arises from the relation between the thing qualified and the thing that qualifies. For instance, when the preception of a jar takes place by the intercourse of an organ of sight, there the intercourse is conjunction. In the preception of the colour of the jar, there the intercourse is the intimate union whith that which is in conjuction, for the colour is intimately united with the jar which is in conjunction with the organ of sight. In the perception of the presence of the generality of colour, there the intercourse is the intimate union with what is intimately united with that which is in conjunction, for in the colour that is intimately united with the jar which is in cojuction with the organ of sight, is inherent in the generic property of being coloured. In the perception of Sound by the organ of hearing, there the intercourse is intimate union, for the ether pervading the cavity of the ear, is the organ of hearing, and sound being the specific quality of ether, and there being an intimate relation between a quality and a thing possessing that quality. In the preception of the generic property of sound, the intercourse is the intimate union with that which is intimately united. In the preception of negation, the intercourse is the union which arises from the relation between the thing qualified and the thing that qualifies, for in the preception that 'this ground is possessed with the negation of a jar' there the ground that is in conjunction with the organ of sense is distinguished by the specific quality of the negation of a jar. Thus the knowledge that is prodneed by these intercourses of six kinds is called perception. The instrumental cause of that perception are the organs of sense. Therefore the organs of sense are acknowledged to be the authority of perception. Thus ends the chapter on Sensation and Perception."

The author then goes on to the chapter on Inference.

INFERENCE.

(38.) "The act of inferring (something unknown from the known data) is called inference."

"An inference is knowledge arrived at from a logical deduction. This consists in the knowledge of a general principle combined with the knowledge that the case in question is one to which it is applicable. For instance, the knowledge that 'this hill is possessed with smoke, which is invariably attended by fire' is a logical primise, the knowledge deduced from which, viz. that 'this hill is fiery' is a logical inference. The genrality of a principle (*Vyapti*) consists in the inseparable connection of one given thing with some other as in the instance that 'wherever there is smoke there is fire.' The existence of the thing which forms the middle term (*Vyapya*) of a Syllogism, in the thing which forms the subject of the conclusion or the minor term (*Paksha*) is called the generality of principle of being in the minor term."

The special cause (instrumental cause) of an inference is the knowledge of the invariable connection of the subject with the predicate in a general proposition (*Vyapti-jnana*)

For instance, let a man who from the smoke on a hearth, &c. has become aware of the invariable connection of smoke with fire, see afterwards any where on a mountain uninterrupted line of smoke. He will then recollect the general proposition that 'smoke is invariably connected with fire.' Hence arises the knowledge, that 'this mountain is possessed with smoke which is invariably connected with fire' thence arises the knowledge that 'this mountain is fiery' which is an inference.

The ancients held, that smoke, when actually perceived, together with the notion, that it is invariably connected with fire, is the special cause of a conclusion. The modern philosophers deny this; for they say, if the reason (*Linga*, sign) were the special cause of the conclusion, then inference could not take place, if the reason (sign) had not yet arrived, or had been destroyed; because then the reason, the pretended special cause of a conclusion, was not present.

It is difficult to find an adequate word for the term (*Vyapti*) in English. It means literally, pervading inherence, the inherent and essential presence of any one thing or property in another, but it is used in the Nyaya and other philosophical systems to denote the logical relation of one notion to another in a proposition of such a kind, that under circumstances an inference may be drawn from it; or it is the relation of the subject to the predicate and vice versa, as the major proposition of a syllogism. The subject of such a proposition is the (*Vyapya*) the notion, which is pervaded by another (by the predicate) that is to say, which is only a part of the predicate, which is less extensive than the latter, or included in it. The subject is therefore invariably connected with the predicate and if the former is thought, the latter also is thought. The predicate is the

(*Vyapaka,*) the pervading notion; it has a greater extent than the subject, and the latter is only a part of it. It is, therefore, not invariably connected with it, and if the predicate is thought, the subject is not necessarily thought with it. The Vyapti is, accordingly, only understood, if the relation of the two notions, to be connected together, on either part is understood. Further, the Vyapti is a proposition, from which an inference can be derived, that is to say, it must be a general proposition, fit to form the major proposition of a Syllogism. The names of Vyapya and Vyapaka are only used with reference to the general proposition ; if a third term (the minor term) is connected with them, they obtain other names, Viz; the Vyapya (middle term) the name of *Hetu*, reason, argument, or *linga*, sign, and the Vyapaka (major term) the name of *Sadhya*, conclusion. The minor term (the subject of the conclusion) is called *Paksha* : place (minor term, subject of the conclusion) viz the place, to be connected by means of the middle term with the major term, or predicate of the conclusion.

The knowledge of the determination of the reason (middle term) which is determined by a general predicate, (major term) in connection with the place (minor term) is the special cause of a conclusion. This can be comprehended in a double manner, either, it is the knowledge, that the subject of the general proposition (the middle term,) is connected with the place (subject of conclusion, minor term) or, it is the knowledge, that the place (subject of conclusion) is possessed of thesubject of the general proposition (middle term.) Accordingly the conclusion takes place either from the knowledge, that the subject of the general proposition (middle term) is connected with the place (subject, minor term) from which follows that the conclusion (predicate of the conclusion, major term) is connected with the place (minor term) or it takes place from the knowledge, that the place (minor term) is possessed of the subjeet of the general proposition (middle term) from which follows, that the place (minor term) is possessed of the conclusion (major term.)

The knowledge of the attribute (middle term) of the subject (of conclusion) as determined by the predicate (major term) with which it is invariably connected takes place through intimate relation, and produces the conclusion by the same relation.

This is on the whole an excellent exposition of the logical relation of the conclusion. It is here lucidly explained in what manner the three notions of a syllogism are in relation to each other, and also that the cause of the conclusion is not the middle term, as separated from the major term, but only in its connection with it. As this is sometimes not attended to, it is not superfluons to attach importance to it. At the same time it is true, that the logical form of a syllogism does not consist of one premise, and the conclusion but of two premises whith one conclusion; for if one reflects as to the form, viz.. the minor term in connection with the middle term, which is itself determined by the major term, it is evident, that there are two connections viz. of the minor term with the middle, and of this with the major. That is to say, there are two propositions or two premises.

(39) "The process of Infernce is of two kinds, for one's own self, and for the sake of others. That which is for one's own self, is the cause of deduction of a logical inference in one's own mind;

for instance, having made repeated and personal observations, in the case of culinary hearths and the like, that wherever there is smoke there is fire, having come to the conclusion, that this an invariable sequence, having reached a mountain, and having entertained a doubt about the existence of fire in it, and having observed smoke on the mountain, a man recollects the invariable and unconditional antecedence of fire, where there is smoke. Afterwards this knowledge arises in his mind that this mountain is distinguished by smoke which is invariably and unconditionally attended by fire. This is called *Linga-paramarsa* which means such recognition of *linga* or sign as leads to a logical inference Thence is produced the knowledge, that the 'mountain is fiery.' This is ealled a logical inference for one's own self."

(40) "But, when any one, after having for the satisfaction of his own mind inferred fire from smoke, makes the application of the five-membered syllogistic form for the edification of the understanding of others, that inference is called the inference for the sake of others. As for instance

I. This hill is fiery.

II Because it smokes.

III. Whatever is possessed of smoke is fiery, as a culinary hearth.

IV. And that it does so.

V. Therefore it is fiery. Thus from a sign already established, the other man also is convinced of the existance of fire."

(41) 'The five-membered (*Avayavas* or propositions) of the syllogistic form are as follows :—

1. The proposition (*pratijna* that which is to be proved by argument)

2. The reason, argument or *hetu* ;

3. The instance (*udaharana, drishtanta*).

4. The application (*upanaya*).

5. The conclusion (*nigamana*).

For instance ;

1. 'This hill is fiery'; is the proposition.

2. 'For it smokes' is the reason or *hetu.*

3. 'Whatever smokes is fiery'; is the instance or *udaharana.*

4. 'This hill smokes'; is the application or *upanaya*

5. 'Therefore it is fiery'; is the conclusion or *nigamana.*

The modern school of the Nyaya has reduced the syllogism to three and even to two members, and this last reduction appears to have been most generally adopted. In this form the two premises, viz. major and minor propositions are condensed into one premise, of which we shall now give a description.

* That a syllogism be correct, two things are required. 1, a general proposition, in which the subject (reason) is invariably connected with a predicate (conclusion), more comprehensive than the subject, and 2, a minor term with which the subject of the general proposition is connected. That there is this double connexion of the minor term with the reason, and of the reason with the conclusion, is to be decided by consideration, which is the intercourse between the minor term and the reason, as connected with the general predicate or the predicate of

the conclusion. This consideration is only one, and therefore the form of the antecedent of the conclusion can only be one, or: there is only one premise, by which the minor term is expressed as determined by the reason in its invariable connexion with the conclusion.

For instance: let a man from former observation know, that smoke is invariably connected with fire, as for instance on a culinary hearth; let him see afterwards an uninterrupted column of smoke rising from a hill, he will recollect the general proposition that smoke is invariably connected with fire. Hence the knowledge arises: This hill is possessed of smoke, which is invariably connected with fire. This knowledge, this one act, by which there is a progress from one object to a third by a second, is consideration, from which the conclusion arises: This hill is fiery.

This is in its principal points the theory of the Nyaya of the form of the syllogism. It is essentially the same with that of Aristotle. The differences are two. The first is a difference in the form, or rather in expression, viz. that the two permises are combined into one. The exposition is certainly not simple, for the different combination of the ideas, forming a syllogism, ought to be represented in their natural form, which is the connexion of two in a proposition, and the same principle ought to have been applied to the conclusion; for if it is true that two premises must be combined into one, the conclusion also should not be stated in a separate sentence, but the whole syllogism should form one sentence, for instance, in the example: This hill, determined by smoke, which is determined by fire, is determined by fire. Yet the difference is only apparent;

for the Nyaya, as Aristotle, connects, one notion with the other through a third with which the latter is connected, or excludes it by a third, from which the second is excluded.

The second difference is, that the Nyaya wanted not only to give rules for the correctness of the logical operation in arguing, but to guard against false premises, and for this purpose the consideration was also to establish the truth of the major proposition by a reference to an instance, in which the truth of the propo-sition was exemplified. Their consideration was therefore, not only directed to the logical operation of arguing, but also to the truth which may result from it, and both the truth of the conclusion, and the correctness of the argument should be the result of one and the same opera-tion, which of course is impossible.

With the exposition of the form of syllogism, the logical theory of the Nayaya is nearly completed. Gautama divided inference into three kinds ; 1, inference of an effect from a cause, as if rain is inferred from a collection of clouds ; 2, inference of a cause from an effect, as if rain is concluded from an increase of the water in a river ; and 3, inference from general notions, as if earth is inferred to be a substance from its having the quality of smell. This division, is not logical, as cause and effect are metaphysical notions and have no relation whatever to the different forms of syllogism. The modern school of the Nayaya has therefore not adopted this division, but acknowledges three kinds of syllogisms; which are only affirmative inference, only negative inference, and inference, at the same time affirmative and negative. From the examples, given in illustration, it appears, that the latter includes two moods of the first and second figures, Barbara and Camestres ; Barbara being the type for all general affirmative conclusions, and Camestres for all gener negative ones. Here, however, is their theory finished and we find no trace of the different moods the syllogistical forms can enter into.

(42) "The(*linga-paramarsa*) or the recognition of a sign is alone the instrumental cause of an inference (*anumiti*), both of that for one's own self and of that for another ; therefore the *linga-paramarsa* or the recognition of a sign is an act of inference (*anumanam*)."

(43) "A Sign (*linga*) is of three kinds, (1) that which has reference to an invariable union and separation (*anwaya-vyatireki*) ; (2) that which has reference to union alone,(*kewalanwayi*)and (3)that which has reference to separation alone (*kewalavyatireki*) ;. Where the sign has reference to the pervading inherence (*Vyapti*) both by union and separation, there the sign is called that which has reference to an inseparable union and separation ; as for instance, the state of being *smoky*, when *fire* is to be proved. 'Wherever there is smoke, there is fire as a culinary hearth'; this an universal affirmative. 'Where there is no fire, there can also be no smoke, as for instance in the case of a great 'lake' ; this an universal negative. The sign which has reference to union alone is that which has no negative *dristanta* or example, as for instance, 'this jar is nameable, because it is cognizable by *prama* or true

apprehension, as cloth is'. For there is no instance where a thing is unnameable when it is cognizable by true apprehension and vice versa. The sign that has a reference to separation alone, is that in regard to which we argue from an invariable absence.

As an example we institute the following syllogism :—

' (1) Earth differs from these (other elements) :

' (2) Because it possesses smell :

'(3) Whatever is not different from these (other elements) is not possessed of smell, as for instance water, (ie it is not possessed of smell) :

'(4) But this (earth) is not so (ie is not unpossessed of smell) :

(5) Therefore it is not like the other elements.

But if (in the the third proposition) we argued (affirmatively) that 'whatever is possessed of smell is different from the other elements,' we would have been in want of an instance to cite, the earth being the singular instance of that."

Without undergoing the needless necessity of citing an example in an argument, it can be simplified by stating a universal affirmative premise thus:—

" 1. Whatever is possessed of smell, differs from the other elements. :

(2) Earth is possessed of smell :

(3) Therefore Earth differs from other elements."

The connexion of the subject with the predicate is two-fold. Namely, there are three kinds of inference, viz; only affirmative, only negative, and affirmative and negative at the same time.

1. The only affirmative kind takes place, when there are no dissimilar instances with regard to the conclusion (major term, that is to say, when the major term is not excluded from any other notion) for instance, if it is argued, that something is an object of knowledge, because it can be named; for here is a dissimilar instance impossible as every thing is an object of knowledge.

If it is said, 'that the only affirmative kind is impossible, because it is separated from all other notions' (that is to say, such a notion is separated from all other notions, and cannot therefore be connected with all.) We deny this; for what is separated, is common to all, and this is merely affirmative. Moreover, the mere affirmation is the notion of a thing which is no object of actual absolute negation, and this is proved in the negation of the ether, &c. (that is to say, as it cannot be proved, that ether, space, &c. are not found any where, so it cannot be proved with regard to such notions as knowledge, &c.).

2. Merely negative inference takes place, when there exist no similar subjects of conclusion, for instance, in the inference: Earth is distinguished from all the other elements, because it is possessed of smell. Here is earth the minor term, the conclusion the distinction from what is different from earth, and reason the smell; for in this case there is no similar instance, viz. no instance with which tbe conclusion is connected, because it was before excluded from the other elements.

3. Affirmative and negative inferences take place, when there exist similar and dissimilar instances of the conclusion or major term; for instance: This is fiery, because it smokes. In this case there are similar instances, as a hearth, &c., and dissimilar instances, as a lake, &c.

The cause of the negative conclusion is the knowledge of a general negative proposition, *Vyatirekavyapti* Hence the true definition of a general negative proposition is this:—A general negative is the necessity of the absence of the reason, where there is an absence of the conclusion or the major term; that is to say, a general negative is the absence of the reason, which absence is included in the absence of the conclusion or major term. Here it must be understood, by what connexion, at what place, and by what notion, the more extensive notion is comprehended, by the same connexion and notion is also the absence to be determined. From this knowledge it follows: by what connexion and notion, the more comprehensive notion is comprehended, by the same connexion and notion is also the absence to be determined. Accordingly, where the absence of smell expresses the notion of the other elements by distinctive relation, there follows the absolute negation of the notion of the other elements by the negation of the negation of smell; but where the more extensive notion of the other elements is comprehended by the relation af identy; this is reciprocal negation. And lastly, when by the relation of conjunction, for instance, the more extensive notion of fire with regard to smoke is comprehended, there the negation of smoke, determined by the relation of conjunction, in a tank also follows from the negation of fire, determined by the relation of conjunction. Here is the cause of the apprehension of the general negative proposition, the knowledge of what agrees with a general negative.

Another opinion on the subject is that: By means of the negative, the general affirmative is understood, but the knowledge of the general negative proposition, is not the cause. Where by means of the general negative, the general proposition is understood, there it is called a negative inference. The necessity of the conclusion (major term, here the difference from the other elements) is first evident from single things, as a jar, &c. and afterwards it is established for the notion of earth, &c.

(44) "That, where the existence of the property to be proved is doubtful, is called the subject of the conclusion (*paksha*); as the mountain, when the fact of its having possessed of smoke is the reason (argument or *hetu*). That, where the existence of the property to be proved is undoubted, is called the subject on the same side or *Sapaksha*; as the culinary hearth, in the same argument. That which is undoubtedly possessed of the negation of the property to be proved, is called the subject in opposition or *vipaksha*; as a great lake in the same argument."

OF FALLACIES.

(45) "There are five semblances of reason or fallacies or *hetwabhasas*, which are as follows :—

I. Going astray.

II. Contradiction.

III. Equalization.

IV. Inconclusiveness.

V. Absurdity."

(46) "The fallacy of going astray or *savyabhichara* is that which may have a conclusion different from that which is wanted.

It is of three kinds.

1. That which is too general or *Sadharana.*

2. that which is not general enough or *asadharana.*

3. And that which is non-exclusive or *anupasanhari.*

The fallacy of going astray, which is too general, is that where the reason or *hetu* may be present, when the property to be proved is absent; as for example, if one would say, 'The mountain is fiery, because it is cognizable by *prama* or true apprehension but cognizability by *prama* or true apprehension can as well be ascribed to a lake which is possessed of the negation of fire.'"

(47) "The fallacy of going astray that is not general enough, is excluded from the subject of conclusion and from an oposite onpe. As for example, 'sound is eternal, because it is possessed of the generic property of souud.' This is a fallacy of going astray that is not general enough, for the generic property of sound exists in sound alone and excluded from all, either eternal or non-eternal."

(47) "The fallacy of going astray that is non-exclusive or *anupasanhari,* where no example can

be brought either in support or in opposition. As for instance, if it is said, that 'Every thing is non-eternal, beeause it is cognizable by *prama* knowledge without error,'—here there is no examplo to cite, because 'every thing' is the subject of the conclusion."

(48) "The fallacy of contradiction or *virudha* is that, where the reason is invariably attended with the negation of what is to be proved. As for example, when it is said that,—'sound is eternal because it is created.' This argument should be rejected as fallacious, because the state of having been created is attended with non-eternity:—the negation of eternity."

(49) "It is called the fallacy of equalization or *satpratipaksha* when the reason is counterbalanced by another reason which proves the negation of what is to be proved. As for example, when one would say that, 'The sound is eternal, because it is cognizable by the organ of hearing, as the generio property of sound is acknowledged by both parties,' it might be said with equal force on the other side, that, 'sound is non-eternal, because it is a creation, as a jar is.'

(50) "The fallacy of inconclusiveness, is of three kinds:—

1. inconclusiveness on the part of the subject *asrayasiddha*;

2. inconclusiveness from the nature of the reason *swarupasidha*;

3. inconclusive-ness from limitation." *(vyapyatwasiddha)*

(51) "As an example of the inconclusiveness on the part of the subject it is cited, 'The sky-lotus is fragrant, because it is possessed of the generic property of lotuses, as in the lotuses of the lake,' here the sky-lotus is the locality of the generic property of a lotus, which sky-lotus is in reality non-existent."

(52) "Inconclusiveness from the nature of the reason takes place, for instance, when it is inferred 'that sound is a quality, because it is cognizable by the organ of sight.' But this cognizability by the organ of sight is not existent in the sound; sound being cognizable by the organ of hearing. Inconclusiveness from limitation would take place, for instance, when the reason is attended with an indispensable condition. Such an indispensable condition or *upadhi* is what always attends the property to be proved, but does not always attend what is brought forward as a proof."

(53) "Invariable attendance on the object to be proved (*sadhya-vyapakatwa*) consists in the not being the counterpart (*apratiyogitwa*) of the absolute negation (*atyantabhava*) attendant on (*samanadhikarana*) that which is to be proved. Non-invariable attendance on that which is cited as a proof (*sadhana-vyapakatwa*) consists in the being th counterpart (*pratiyogitwa*) of the negation which exists in the proof."

(54) "In the argument that, 'The mountain is possessed of smoke, because it has fire,' here the contact of wet fuel is an indispensable condition. As for instance, 'wherever there is smoke there is the union with wet fuel,' is an invariable attendance on what is to be proved (*sadhyavyapakata*). But such an inference is not true, 'That wherever there is fire, there is the union with wet fuel' for there is no union with wet fuel in the case of an ignited iron ball—this is what is called the non-invariable attendance on the proof or *sadhana-vaypakata*. Thus the invariable attendance on what is [to be proved being coexistent with the non-invariable attendace on the proof, the indispensable condition there is the nnion with wet fuel. As this additional condition is indispensable here, to prove the absolute presence of smoke, fieriness in this argument is fallacious as regards its conclusiveness."

Such an argument as expressed in the form, 'The mountain is fiery :—therefore it mnst have smoke,' is called an Enthymeme, because here of the two premises of a regular syllogism only one is expressed and the other is suppressed in the mind *(en thymo)* of the speaker. When a fallacy occurs in an Enthymeme, it is very difficult to detect whether the fallacy is in the reasoning or it is a fallacy *extra dictionem.*

(55) "The fallacy of absurdity or *badhita,* is that where the negation of what is to be proved is established without doubt by another proof. If for example, one would say that, ' Fre is cold,

because it is a substance.' Here the predicate of the conclusion, what is to be proved, is coldness, the negation of which, warmth, is apprehended by the organ of touch by one's own self. Hence the argument is called absurd."

"Thus ends the chapter on Inference."

Too general is a reason, which abides as well in the subject of the concusion as in an oposite one; subject of the conclusion (*sapaksha*) is, where the major term abides, for instance, if fire is the major, smoke the middle, a mountain or a hearth is the subject or the minor &c. A subject opposite to the conclusion (*Vipaksha*) is, where it does not abide; for instance, in the example given above, a tank is a subject, opposite to the conclusion or the major term,

That is to say, the reason is too general, when it abides *also* in a subject, where the major term is not found. For instance, let a hearth be the subject or minor term; smoke the major term, and fire the reason, the conclusion would be: the hearth smokes, because it is fiery, which would be false, because it is too general; for fire, the reason, is also connected with other subjects, where there is no smoke, for instance, with an ignited iron ball.

This is not a *logical fallacy*, which takes place, when the conclusion does not follow from the premises but as a fallaey *extra dictionem*, where the matter of the permises is wrong; for the conclusion follows here from the premises. In this instance the major proposition is wrong, which is: wherever there is fire there is smoke. The conclusion, however, is quite right as well in form as in matter, and the example is therefore not judiciously selected. The fault would, however be apparent, if iron ball for instance had been taken for the minor term.

Non-general is the reason, which has no similar subjects of conclusion for the major term, that is where the major term has only one subject, or where no similar instances can be adduced for the reason.

Non-exclusive, is a reason, where the major term is the negation of absolute negation ie where the major term may be predicated of any other notion. Hereby a general negative is impossible and a conclusion therefore cannot take place.

A contradictory reason is one which does dot abide in the subject of conclusion or minor term, that is to say, a reason, whose negation is the major term or reason which is the contrary notion of the major term. Be cow the subject, the notion (class) of cow the major, and the notion of horse the middle term. Here the reason, the notion of the horse, excludes the major, the notion of cow, and therefore does not admit of an inference. Here the fault is in the reasoning, but the major premise is wrong; it is therefore a fallacy *extra dictionem*.

1. Inconclusiveness on the part of the subject is there, where the notion of the subject or the minor term, is impossible

For instance, if it should be inferred, that a golden-hill is fiery, the conclusion could not take place, because there is no such thing as a golden hill.

Here also the conclusion is not wrong, the fault lies in the minor premise, where the subject is a notion, not given by experience; and the fallacy is therefore one *extra dictionem*.

2. Inconclusiveness from the nature of the reason or the middle term, takes place, if the reason is not found in the subject, with which a connexion was supposed if the reason and the subject exclude each other. Let it for instance be argued that a tank is a thing, because, it smokes. Tank or water in the tank, and smoke are contrary notions, and smoke therefore cannot be predicated of a tank.

Here also lies the fallacy in the minor premise. We observe, that the second kind of inconclusiveness does not correspond to the first. In the first the minor term, was contradictory, and we should therefore have expected, that in the second the reason would have been contradictory.

3. Inconclusiveness from limitation on the part of the invariable connexion with the predicate. This can be two-fold, on the part of the suject, and on the part of the predicate.

a. On the part of the predicate. This takes place if the predicate is a contradictory notion. For instance, if the inference were made, that the mountain has a golden fire, the notion of a golden fire, major term is contradictory.

Here the major premise is wrong,

b. Secondly on the part of the reason. This takes place, if the reason is contradictory, for instance, if the argument were 'the mountain is fiery from golden smoke.' The fault is here again in the major premise.

Some say, that this kind takes place, if the terms are too narrow, as if it should be inferred that the mountain is fiery, because it has blue smoke.

IV. An equalised reason is the consideration of opposite reasons. An equalised reason takes place, if at the time of the consideration of a reason, invariably connected with the absence of the conclusion or the major term the consideration of a reason occurs with which the conclusion is invariably connected; as for instance, if at the time of consideration of water, &c. which is invariably connected with the absence of fire,there is a consideration of smoke invariably connected with fire.

V. Absurdity is, if a subject is without the conclusion, which is assigned to it.

Absurdity takes place, if the conclusion does not abide in the subject or minor term; for instance, if at the time of the production of a jar, the jar is taken as the subject or minor term, and smell as the conclusion, there is an absurdity, because at the time of production there is no smell in a jar, &c. for all things are at that time without smell.

COMPARISON.

(56) " Comparison (*upamaina*) is the instrumental cause of the act of comparing (two or more things with one another from similarity). The act of comparing is the knowledge of the relation which exists between a name and a thing named. The cause of this is a knowledge of similarity. The recollection of the extension of the signification of a word by analogy is a step involved in the operation. As for instance a man not knowing what is signified by

the word *gavaya* (Bos gavaeus), and having heard from a forest-man that '*a gavaya* is like a cow' resorts to a forest, where having recollected the meaning of the sentence told to him, he sees a body like that of a cow. Then arises this act of comparison in his mind, that, 'this is what is meant by the word *gavaya*.' "

"Thus has comparison been explained."

The author then goes on to the chapter on Testimony.

TESTIMONY.

(57) "A word is an assertion by one worthy of trust. He is but called worthy of trust, who speaks the truth. A sentence is a collection of significant sounds; as for instance, 'Bring the cow.' A significant sound or *pada* is that which has the power to convey a certain meaning. 'This meaning is to be understood from this significant sound' is the will of God, which is called the convention or the power."

(58) "Mutual correspondence, compatibilty, and juxtaposition of the words are (unitedly) the cause of the knowledge of the significance of a sentence."

These three requisites are elucidated below.

(59) "The reverse of a tendency to convey any other than the intended connexion of one word with another, is what is called the mutual correspondence (*akanksha*). Compatabality (*yogyata*) is nothing more than the non-futility of the signification of a sen-

tence. Juxtaposition (*sannidhi*) is the pronunciation of words without long pause (between each)."

The want of the three requisites enumerated above are examplified below.

(60) "A sentence or a collection af words wanting in mutual correspondence, &c., is no valid sentence—for instance, 'cow, horse, man, elephant,' gives no proof, there being no mutual reference between the words."

Akanksha literally means desiring for, or looking after something. In the sentence: '*Dittha chadram pasyati*,' or '*Dittha* (an individual) sees the moon,' here the word 'Dittha' being in the nominative case, wants a verb to regulate, which it finds in the word 'pasyati.' Again the verb 'pasyati' requires an action to govern which it finds in the word 'chandram,' similarly the word 'chandram' requires a nominative and a verb which it finds in 'Dittha' and 'pasyati.' Thus there is a mutual correspondence between the three words, 'Dittha' 'chandram' and 'pasyati.' The author then goes on to show that mutual correspondence alone is not sufficient to make a sentence valid.

As for instance :—

(61) "The sentence 'He should irrigate with fire' is not valid, as it is in want of compatibility (there being no such thing between fire and irrigation, water alone being compatible with irrigation.)"

This is an instance where though there is no want of mutual correspondence or *akanksha*, yet the sentence is not valid as there is no compatibility or *yogyata* between fire and irrigation. The Author then shows how a sen-ence may not be valid, though it may be complete as regards mutual correspondence and compatibility, if it is in want of the juxtaposition of the words in it.

(62) "Words pronounced not close together but at intervals of *praharas* (or two and half hours of the solar day), such as 'Bring—the—cow' &c. form no valid sentences, as there is a want of the juxtaposition of the words."

This is an instance of the invalidity of a sentence owing to the absence of juxtaposition of the words constituting it, though it is valid as regards its mutual correspodence and compatability.

(63) "Speech is of two kinds, divine (*vaidika*), and human (*laukika*). What is called *vaidika* or divine is authoritative as it is uttered by God. But human or *laukika* speech, that is uttered by one who deserves confidence, is alone authoritative; other is not so."

(64) "The knowledge of the meaning of a sentence is verbal knowledge (*sabdabodha*). Its special cause is (the knowledge of) words. Thus is ascertained what is called True Apprehension."

FALSE APPREHENSION.

(65) False apprehension is of three kinds, through the division of doubt, mistake, and the fault of *reductio ad absurdum*."

(66) "The recognition, in a thing possessing a certain quality, of many contradictory qualities as characterising it, is doubt or *Sansaya*. For instance 'whether a post or a man.'"

Darkness or insufficient light is the cause of this doubt.. When we do not come to a resolution, whether this is *not* a post, or this is *not* a man, and we confound the qualities of both in it, it is then called *doubt.*

(67) "False knowledge is mistake or *viparyaya*. For instance, the knowledge of silver in a pearl-shell."

(68) "*Reductio ad absurdum* or *tarka* is that which consists in founding the pervader (here supposed to be denied) through the allegation of the pervaded (here supposed to be taken for granted). As for instance, 'If there were not fire (which you do not grant), then there would not be smoke (which you admit there is)."

(69) "Memory is also two-fold, true and false. True memory is that which arises from true apprehension. False memory is that which arises from false apprehension."

The author having exhausted the subject of Intellect, hurries on to the remaing qualities of pleasure pain, &c.

(70) "That is called pleasure or *sukham* which is agreeable to the perception of all; likewise that is called pain or *dukham* which is disagreeable (to the preception of all)."

(71) "Desire or *ichcha* means wishing. Aversion or *dwesha* means wishing-ill-of. Effort (*prayatna*) means action."

(72) "Virtue or merit (*dharma*) arises from the performance of what is enjoined; but what is called vice or demerit (*adharma*) is that which arises from the perpetration of what is prohibited."

(73) "The eight qualities, commencing from intellect, are the specific qualities of soul alone."

(74) "Intellect, desire, and effort, are of two kinds eternal and non-eternal or transient. These are eternal when they belong to God, and non-eternal or transient when they appertain to mortals."

(75) "Faculty is of three kinds, velocity, thought, and elasticity. Velocity or *vega* abides in the four substances beginning with Earth and in mind. Thought or *bhavana* which arises from perception and is the cause of memory, exists in soul alone. Elasticity or *sthitisthapaka* is the restorer to former position, of a thing whose position has been changed, and is a quality that abides in mats and such other substances formed of earthly elements."

"Thus ends the chapter on the Qualities."

The author then goes on to the category of Action.

ACTION.

(76) "Action consists in motion."

Casting upward or *utkshepana* is the cause of a contact with the higher region. Casting downwards or *apakshepana* is the cause of contact with a lower region. Contraction or *akunchana* is the cause of the close contact with what is near to the body. Dilation or *prasarana* is the cause of the close contact with what is distant. Every thing else is called going or *gamana*. Action exists in the four substances beginning from the earth and in the mind."

The author then proceeds to the category of genus or generality.

GENUS OR GENERALITY.

(77) "Genus or Genrality (*samanya*) is eternal, one and belonging to many, and abiding in Substance, Quality, and Action. It is two-fold, higher and lower. The highest degree of genus or generality or the *Summum genus* is existence. The lower degree is called the species or *jati*, such as is substantiality or the common nature of what are called substances."

Of the two *para* and *apara*, *para* is that which is more extensive and therefore is called the *Genus*.; and *apara* is less extensive and therefore is called the *species*

The author then goes on to the category of Particularity.

PARTICULARITY.

(78) "Particularities or *viseshas* are existent in, eternal substances and are such that they exclude (the eternal substances) from each other."

Eternal substances are 1. mind, 2 soul, 3 time, 4 space 5 ether; and 6 the atoms of earth, water, and air. Then comes the category of Intimate Relation.

INTIMATE RELATION.

(79) "Intimate relation or *samavaya* is eternal connexion. It abides in things which can not exist separately. Two things which can not exist separately are those, of which two, one exists as absorbed in the other. Such pairs are, parts and whole composed of those parts, qualities and the thing qualified, action and actor, species and individual, particularity and eternal substances."

At last the author comes to the last of the categories ie negation or non-existence.

NEGATION.

(80) "It is of various sorts. Antecedent negation or *pragabhava* is without beginning, but has a termination. Such is the negation of an action before it is produced. Destruction or *pradhwansa* has a beginning, but no termination. Such is the negation of an action subsequent to its production. Absolute negation or *atyantabhava* is the counterpart of what is distinguished by union during the three times past, present and future. As for example, 'There is no jar on the ground.' Mutial negation or *anyonyabhava* is the counterpart of what is distinguished by union with identy. As for instance. 'A jar cannot be cloth.'

(81) "Since every thing is included under the categories enumerated, categories are therefore ascertained to be seven alone."

The author concludes with the following couplet:—

(82) "These logical and philosophical aphorisoms were composed by the learned *Anna Bhatta*, in order to clear the understanding of juvinile students as regards the opinions of *Kanada* and of *Nayaya*."

Gotama is the founder of *nyaya* or logic ; and *kanada* is the founder of the system of philosophy called *vaiseshika*.

"Thus is the *Traka Sangraha* finished."

तर्कसंग्रहः।

१। निधाय हृदि विश्वेशं विधाय गुरुवन्दनम्।
बालानां सुखबोधाय क्रियते तर्कसंग्रहः॥

२। द्रव्यगुणकर्मसामान्यविशेषसमवायाभावाः सप्तपदार्थाः।

३। तत्र द्रव्याणि पृथिव्यप्तेजो वाय्वाकाशकालदिगात्ममनांसि नवैव।

४। रूपरसगन्धस्पर्शसंख्यापरिमाणपृथक्त्वसंयोगविभागपरत्वापरत्वगुरुत्वद्रवत्वस्नेहशब्दबुद्धिसुखदुःखेच्छाद्वेषप्रयत्नधर्माधर्मसंस्काराश्चतुर्विंशतिर्गुणाः।

५। उत्क्षेपणावक्षेपणाकुञ्चनप्रसारणगमनानि पञ्चैव कर्म्माणि।

६। परमपरञ्चेति द्विविधं सामान्यम्।

नित्यद्रव्यवृत्तयो विशेषास्त्वनन्ता एव।

७। समवायस्त्वेक एव।

अभावश्चतुर्विधः प्रागभावः प्रध्वंसाभावोऽत्यन्ताभावोऽन्योन्याभावश्चेति।

८। तत्र गन्धवती पृथिवी सा द्विविधा नित्याऽनित्या चेति नित्या परमाणुरूपा। अनित्या कार्यरूपा। सा पुनस्त्रिविधा शरीरेन्द्रियविषयभेदात्। शरीरमस्मदादीनाम् इन्द्रियं गन्धग्राहकं घ्राणं तच्च नासाग्रवर्त्ति विषयो मृत्पाषाणादिः।

९। शीतस्पर्शवत्य आपः।

ताश्च द्विविधा नित्या अनित्याश्च। नित्याः परमाणुरूपाः। अनित्याः कार्यरूपाः। ताः पुनस्त्रिविधाः शरीरेन्द्रियविषयभेदात्। शरीरं वरुणलोके। इन्द्रियं रसग्राहकं रसनं तच्च जिह्वाग्रवर्त्ति। विषयः सरित्समुद्रादिः॥

१०। उष्णस्पर्शवत्तेजः। तद्द्विविधं नित्यमनित्यञ्च। नित्यं परमाणुरूपम् अनित्यं कार्यरूपम्। पुनस्त्रिविधं शरीरेन्द्रियविषयभेदात्। शरीरमादित्यलोके प्रसिद्धम्। इन्द्रियं रूपग्राहकं चक्षुः तच्च कृष्णताराग्रवर्त्ति। विषयश्चतुर्विधो भौमदिव्यौदर्याकरजभेदात्। भौमं वह्न्यादिकम्।

अविन्धनं दिव्यं विद्युदादि । भुक्तस्य परिणामहेतुरौदर्यम् । आकरजं सुवर्णादि ।

११ । रूपरहितस्पर्शवान्वायुः । स द्विविधो नित्योऽनित्यश्च । नित्यः परमाणुरूपोऽनित्यः कार्यरूपः । पुनस्त्रिविधः शरीरेन्द्रियविषयभेदात् । शरीरं वायुलोके । इन्द्रियं स्पर्शग्राहकं त्वक् तच्च सर्वशरीरवर्त्ति । विषयो वृक्षादिकम्पनहेतुः ॥

१२ । शरीरान्तः सञ्चारी वायुः प्राणः स चैकोऽप्युपाधिभेदात्प्राणापानादिसंज्ञां लभते ॥

१३ । शब्दगुणकमाकाशं तच्चैकं विभु नित्यञ्च । अतीतादिव्यवहारहेतुः कालः स चैको विभुर्नित्यश्च ।

१४ । प्राच्यादिव्यवहारहेतुर्दिक् सा चैका नित्या विभ्वी च ।

१५ । ज्ञानाधिकरणमात्मा । स द्विविधो जीवात्मा परमात्मा च । तत्रेश्वरः सर्वज्ञः परमात्मा एक एव सुखदुःखादिरहितः । जीवात्मा प्रतिशरीरं भिन्नो विभुर्नित्यश्च ।

१६ । सुखदुःखाद्युपलब्धिसाधनमिन्द्रियं मनः ।

तच्च प्रत्यात्मनियतत्वादनन्तं परमाणुरूपं नित्यञ्च।

१७। अथ गुणाः।

चक्षुर्मात्रग्राह्यो गुणो रूपम्। तच्च शुक्लनीलपीतरक्तहरितकपिशचित्रभेदात्सप्तविधं पृथिवीजलतेजोवृत्तिः। तत्र पृथिव्यां सप्तविधम्। अभास्वरं शुक्लं जले। भास्वरं शुक्लञ्च तेजसि।

१८। रसनग्राह्यो गुणो रसः। स च मधुराम्ललवणकटुकषायतिक्तभेदात् षड्विधः पृथिवीजलवृत्तिः। पृथिव्यां षड्विधः जले मधुर एव।

१९। घ्राणग्राह्यो गुणो गन्धः। स च द्विविधः सुरभिरसुरभिश्च पृथिवीमात्रवृत्तिः।

२०। त्वगिन्द्रियमात्रग्राह्यो गुणः स्पर्शः। स च त्रिविधः शीतोष्णानुष्णाशीतभेदात् पृथिव्यप्तेजोवायुवृत्तिः। तत्र शीतो जले। उष्णस्तेजसि। अनुष्णाशीतः पृथिवीवाय्वोः।

२१। रूपादिचतुष्टयं पृथिव्यां पाकजमनित्यञ्च। अन्यत्रापाकजं नित्यमनित्यञ्च। नित्यगतं नित्यम्। अनित्यगतमनित्यम्।

२२। एकादिव्यवहारासाधारणहेतुस्संख्या। सा नवद्रव्यवृत्तिः। एकादिपरार्द्धपर्य्यन्ता। एकत्वन्नित्यमनित्यञ्च नित्यगतन्नित्यमनित्यगतमनित्यम्। द्वित्वादिकन्तु सर्वत्रा नित्यमेव।

२३। मानव्यवहारासाधारणं कारणं परिमाणं नवद्रव्यवृत्तिः। तच्च चतुर्विधं अणु महद् दीर्घं ह्रस्वञ्चेति।

२४। पृथग्व्यवहारासाधारणं कारणं पृथक्त्वं सर्वद्रव्यवृत्तिः।

२५। संयुक्तव्यवहारासाधारणो हेतुः संयोगः सर्वद्रव्यवृत्तिः।

२६। संयोगनाशको गुणो विभागः सर्वद्रव्यवृत्तिः।

परापरव्यवहारासाधारणकारणे परत्वापरत्वे। पृथिव्यादिचतुष्टयमनोवृत्तिनी ते द्विविधे दिक्कृते कालकृते च। दूरस्थे दिक्कृतम्परत्वं समीपस्थे दिक्कृतमपरत्वम्। ज्येष्ठे कालकृतम् परत्वं कनिष्ठे कालकृतमपरत्वम्।

२७। आद्यपतनासमवायिकारणं गुरुत्वं पृथिवीजलवृत्तिः।

२८। आद्यस्यन्दनासमवायिकारणं द्रवत्वं पृथिव्यप्तेजोवृत्तिः। तद्द्विविधं सांसिद्धिकं नैमित्तिकञ्च। सांसिद्धिकं जले। नैमित्तिकं पृथिवीतेजसोः। पृथिव्यां घृतादौ अग्निसंयोगजन्यं द्रवत्वम्।

२९। चूर्णादिपिण्डीभावहेतुर्गुणः स्नेहो जलमात्रवृत्तिः।

३०। श्रोत्रग्राह्यो गुणःशब्द आकाशमात्रवृत्तिः। स द्विविधःध्वन्यात्मको वर्णात्मकश्चेति। ध्वन्यात्मको भेर्यादौ। वर्णात्मकःसंस्कृतभाषादिरूपः।

३१। सर्वव्यवहारहेतुर्बुद्धिर्ज्ञानम्।

सा द्विविधा स्मृतिरनुभवश्च।

संस्कारमात्रजन्यं ज्ञानं स्मृतिः। तद्भिन्नं ज्ञानमनुभवः। स द्विविधो यथार्थोऽयथार्थश्च।

३२। तद्वति तत्प्रकारकानुभवो यथार्थः यथा रजते इदं रजतमिति ज्ञानम्। सैव प्रमेत्युच्यते। तदभाववति तत्प्रकारको ऽनुभवो ऽयथार्थः। यथा शुक्ताविदं रजतमित्यादि ज्ञानम्।

३३। यथार्थानुभवश्चतुर्विधः प्रत्यक्षानुमित्युपमितिशाब्दभेदात्। तत्करणमपि चतुर्विधं प्रत्यक्षानुमानोपमानशब्दभेदात्।

३४। व्यापारवदसाधारणं कारणं करणम्।
अनन्यथासिद्धकार्यनियतपूर्ववृत्तिः कारणम्।
कार्यं प्रागभावप्रतियोगि।

३५। कारणं त्रिविधं समवाय्यसमवायिनिमित्तभेदात्। यत्समवेतं कार्यमुत्पद्यते तत्समवायि कारणं यथा तन्तवः पटस्य, पटश्च स्वगतरूपादेः। कार्येण कारणेन वा सहैकस्मिन्नर्थे समवेतत्वे सति कारणम्, असमवायि कारणं यथा तन्तुसंयोगःपटस्य, तन्तुरूपं पटरूपस्य। तदुभयभिन्नं कारणं निमित्तकारणं यथा तुरीवेमादिकं पटस्य। तदेतत्त्रिविधकारणमध्ये यदसाधारणं कारणं तदेव करणम्।

३६। तत्र प्रत्यक्षज्ञानकरणं प्रत्यक्षम्। इन्द्रियार्थसन्निकर्षजन्यं ज्ञानं प्रत्यक्षम्। तत् द्विविधं निर्विकल्पकं सविकल्पकञ्च। तत्र निष्प्रकारकं ज्ञानं निर्विकल्पकम्। यथा इदं किञ्चित्। स-

प्रकारकं ज्ञानं सविकल्पकम् । यथा डित्थो-ऽयम् । ब्राह्मणोऽयम् । श्यामोऽयमिति ।

३७ । प्रत्यक्षज्ञानहेतुरिन्द्रियार्थसन्निकर्षः षड्विधः संयोग, संयुक्तसमवाय, संयुक्तसमवेतसमवाय, समवाय, समवेतसमवाय, विशेषणविशेष्यभावा इति । चक्षुषा घटप्रत्यक्षजनने संयोगः सन्निकर्षः, घटरूपप्रत्यक्षजनने संयुक्तसमवायः सन्निकर्षः, चक्षुःसंयुक्ते घटे रूपस्य समवायात् । रूपत्वसामान्यप्रत्यक्षे संयुक्तसमवेतसमवायः सन्निकर्षः, चक्षुःसंयुक्ते घटे रूपं समवेतं तत्र रूपत्वस्य समवायात् । श्रोत्रेण शब्दसाक्षात्कारे समवायः सन्निकर्षः, कर्णविवरवृत्त्याकाशस्य श्रोत्रत्वात् शब्दस्याकाशगुणत्वात् गुणगुणिनोश्च समवायात् । शब्दत्वसाक्षात्कारे समवेतसमवायः सन्निकर्षः, श्रोत्रसमवेते शब्दे शब्दत्वस्य समवायात् । अभावप्रत्यक्षे विशेषणविशेष्यभावः सन्निकर्षः, घटाभाववद्भूतलमित्यत्र चक्षुःसंयुक्ते भूतले घटाभावस्य विशेषणत्वात् । एवं सन्निकर्षषट्कजन्यं

ज्ञानं प्रत्यक्षम्। तत्करणं इन्द्रियं तस्मादिन्द्रियं प्रत्यक्षप्रमाणमिति सिद्धम्।

३८। अनुमितिकरणमनुमानम्। परामर्शजन्यं ज्ञानमनुमितिः। व्याप्तिविशिष्टपक्षधर्मताज्ञानं परामर्शः। यथा वह्निव्याप्यधूमवानयं पर्वत इति ज्ञानं परामर्शः। तज्जन्यं पर्वतो वह्निमानिति ज्ञानम् अनुमितिः। यत्र यत्र धूमस्तत्राग्निरिति साहचर्यनियमो व्याप्तिः। व्याप्यस्य पर्वतादिवृत्तित्वं पक्षधर्मता।

३९। अनुमानं द्विविधं स्वार्थं परार्थञ्च। स्वार्थं स्वानुमितिहेतुः। तथाहि। स्वयमेव भूयो भूयो दर्शनेन यत्र यत्र धूमस्तत्राग्निरिति महानसादौ व्याप्तिं गृहीत्वा पर्वतसमीपं गत्वा तद्गते चाग्नौ सन्दिहानः पर्वते धूमं पश्यन् व्याप्तिं स्मरति यत्र धूमस्तत्राग्निरिति। तदनन्तरं वह्निव्याप्यधूमवान् अयं पर्वत इति ज्ञानमुत्पद्यते। अयमेव लिङ्गपरामर्श इत्युच्यते। तस्मात्पर्वतो वह्निमानिति ज्ञानमनुमितिरुत्पद्यते। तदेतत्स्वार्थानुमानम्।

४०। यत्तु स्वयं धूमादग्निमनुमाय परम्प्रति बोध-

यितुं पञ्चावयववाक्यं प्रयुङ्क्ते तत्परार्थानुमानम्। यथा पर्वतो वह्निमान् धूमवत्त्वात्। यो यो धूमवान् स वह्निमान् यथा महानसः। तथा चायम्। तस्मात्तथेति। अनेन प्रतिपादिताल्लिङ्गात्परोऽपि प्रतिपद्यते।

४१। प्रतिज्ञाहेतूदाहरणोपनयनिगमनानि पञ्चावयवाः। पर्वतो वह्निमानिति प्रतिज्ञा। धूमवत्त्वादिति हेतुः। यो यो धूमवानित्युदाहरणम्। तथा चायमित्युपनयः। तस्मात्तथेति निगमनम्॥

४२। स्वार्थानुमितिपरार्थानुमित्योर्लिङ्गपरामर्श एव करणं तस्माल्लिङ्गपरामर्शोऽनुमानम्।

४३। लिङ्गं त्रिविधं अन्वयव्यतिरेकि, केवलान्वयि, केवलव्यतिरेकि चेति। अन्वयेन व्यतिरेकेण च व्याप्तिमदन्वयव्यतिरेकि, यथा वह्नौ साध्ये धूमवत्त्वम्। यत्र धूमस्तत्राग्निर्यथा महानस इत्यन्वयव्याप्तिः। यत्र वह्निर्नास्ति तत्र धूमोऽपि नास्ति यथा ह्रद इति व्यतिरेकव्याप्तिः। अन्वयमात्रव्याप्तिकं केवलान्वयि यथा घटोऽभिधेयः प्रमेयत्वात् पटवत्। अत्र प्रमेयत्वाभिधेयत्वव्या-

तिरेकव्याप्तिर्नास्ति सर्वस्य प्रमेयत्वादभिधेयत्वाच्च । व्यतिरेकमात्रव्याप्तिकं केवलव्यतिरेकि । यथा पृथिवीतरेभ्यो भिद्यते गन्धवत्त्वात् । यदितरेभ्यो न भिद्यते न तद्गन्धवत् यथा जलम् । न चायं तथा । तस्मान्न तथेति । अत्र यद्गन्धवत्तदितरभिन्नमित्यन्वयो दृष्टान्तो नास्ति पृथिवीमात्रस्य पक्षत्वात् ।

४४ । सन्दिग्धसाध्यवान्पक्षः । यथा धूमवत्त्वे हेतौ पर्वतः । निश्चितसाध्यवान् सपक्षः । यथा तत्रैव महानसः । निश्चितसाध्याभाववान् विपक्षः । यथा तत्रैव महाह्रदः ।

४५ । सव्यभिचारविरुद्धसत्प्रतिपक्षासिद्धबाधिताः पञ्च हेत्वाभासाः ।

४६ । सव्यभिचारोऽनैकान्तिकः । स त्रिविधः साधारणासाधारणानुपसंहारिभेदात् । तत्र साध्याभाववद्वृत्तिः साधारणोऽनैकान्तिकः । यथा पर्वतो वह्निमान् प्रमेयत्वादिति प्रमेयत्वस्य वह्न्यभाववति ह्रदे विद्यमानत्वात् ।

४७ । सर्वसपक्षविपक्षव्यावृत्तोऽसाधारणः । यथा शब्दो नित्यः शब्दत्वादिति शब्दत्वं सर्वेभ्यो

नित्येभ्योऽनित्येभ्यश्च व्यावृत्तं शब्दमात्रवृत्तिः । अन्वयव्यतिरेकदृष्टान्तरहितोऽनुपसंहारी यथा सर्वमनित्यं प्रमेयत्वादिति । अत्र सर्वस्यापि पक्षत्वात् दृष्टान्तो नास्ति ।

४८ । साध्याभावव्याप्तो हेतुर्विरुद्धः । यथा शब्दो नित्यः कृतकत्वादिति । कृतकत्वं हि नित्यत्वाभावेनानित्येन व्याप्तम् ।

४९ । साध्याभावसाधकं हेत्वन्तरं यस्य सः सत्प्रतिपक्षः । यथा शब्दो नित्यः श्रावणत्वात् शब्दत्ववदिति । शब्दोऽनित्यः कार्यत्वात् घटवदिति ।

५० । असिद्धस्त्रिविधः । आश्रयासिद्धः स्वरूपासिद्धो व्याप्यत्वासिद्धश्चेति ।

५१ । आश्रयासिद्धो यथा गगनारविन्दं सुरभि अरविन्दत्वात् । सरोजारविन्दवत् । अत्र गगनारविन्दमाश्रयः स च नास्त्येव ।

५२ । स्वरूपासिद्धो यथा शब्दो गुणश्चाक्षुषत्वात् । अत्र चाक्षुषत्वं शब्दे नास्ति शब्दस्य श्रावणत्वात् । सोपाधिको हेतुर्व्याप्यत्वासिद्धः । साध्यव्यापकत्वे सति साधनाव्यापक उपाधिः ।

५३ । साध्यसमानाधिकरणात्यन्ताभावाप्रतियो-

गित्वं साध्यव्यापकत्वम्। साधनवन्निष्ठात्यन्ताभावप्रतियोगित्वं साधनाव्यापकत्वम्।

५४। पर्वतो धूमवान् वह्निमत्त्वादित्यत्राआर्द्रेन्धनसंयोग उपाधिः। तथाहि यत्र धूमस्तत्रार्द्रेन्धनसंयोग इति साध्यव्यापकता। यत्र वह्निस्तत्रार्द्रेन्धनसंयोगो नास्ति अयोगोलके आर्द्रेन्धनसंयोगाभावादिति साधनाव्यापकता। एवं साध्यव्यापकत्वे सति साधनाव्यापकत्वादार्द्रेन्धनसंयोग उपाधिः। सोपाधिकत्वाद्वह्निमत्त्वं व्याप्यत्वासिद्धम्।

५५। यस्य साध्याभावः प्रमाणान्तरेण निश्चितः स बाधितः। यथा वह्निरनुष्णो द्रव्यत्वादिति। अत्रानुष्णत्वं साध्यं तदभाव उष्णत्वं स्पार्शनप्रत्यक्षेण गृह्यते इति बाधितत्वम्। व्याख्यातमनुमानम्॥

५६। उपमितिकरणमुपमानम्। संज्ञासंज्ञिसम्बन्धज्ञानमुपमितिः। तत्करणं सादृश्यज्ञानम्। अतिदेशवाक्यार्थस्मरणमवान्तरव्यापारः। तथाहि गवयशब्दवाच्यमजानन् कुतश्चिदारण्यकपुरुषाद्गोसदृशो गवय इति

श्रुत्वा वनं गतो वाक्यार्थं स्मरन् गोसदृशमपिण्डं पश्यति तदनन्तरं असौ गवयशब्दवाच्य इत्युपमितिरुत्पद्यते ॥ व्याख्यातमुपमानम् ॥

५७। आप्तवाक्यं शब्दः। आप्तस्तु यथार्थवक्ता। वाक्यं पदसमूहः। यथा गामानयेति। शक्तं पदम्। अस्मात्पदादयमर्थो बोद्धव्य इति ईश्वरेच्छा संकेतः शक्तिः।

५८। आकाङ्क्षा योग्यता सन्निधिश्च वाक्यार्थ-ज्ञानहेतुः।

५९। पदस्य पदान्तरव्यतिरेकप्रयुक्तान्वयाननुभावकत्वमाकाङ्क्षा। अर्थाबाधो योग्यता। पदानामविलम्बेनोच्चारणं सन्निधिः।

६०। आकाङ्क्षादिरहितं वाक्यमप्रमाणं यथा गौरश्वः पुरुषो हस्तीति न प्रमाणमाकाङ्क्षाविरहात् ॥

६१। अग्निना सिञ्चेदिति न प्रमाणं योग्यता-विरहात्।

६२। प्रहरे प्रहरे असहोच्चारितानि गामा-नयेत्यादिपदानि न प्रमाणं सान्निध्याभावात्।

६३। वाक्यं द्विविधं वैदिकं लौकिकञ्च। वैदि-

कमीश्वरोक्तत्वात्सर्वमेव प्रमाणम् । लौकिकन्तु आप्तोक्तम्प्रमाणम् अन्यदप्रमाणम् ।

६४ । वाक्यार्थज्ञानं शाब्दज्ञानं तत्करणं शब्दः । इति यथार्थानुभवो निरूपितः ।

६५ । अयथार्थानुभवस्त्रिविधः संशयविपर्यय-तर्कभेदात् ।

६६ । एकस्मिन्धर्मिणि विरुद्धनानाधर्मवैशिष्ट्या-वगाहि ज्ञानं संशयः । यथा स्थाणुर्वा पुरुषो वेति ।

६७ । मिथ्याज्ञानं विपर्ययः । यथा शुक्ताविदं रजतमिति ।

६८ । व्याप्यारोपेण व्यापकारोपस्तर्कः । यथा यदि वह्निर्न स्यात्तर्हि धूमोऽपि न स्यादिति ।

६९ । स्मृतिरपि द्विविधा यथार्था अयथार्था च । प्रमाजन्या यथार्था । अप्रमाजन्याऽयथार्था ।

७० । सर्वेषामनुकूलवेदनीयं सुखम् । प्रति-कूलवेदनीयं दुःखम् ।

७१ । इच्छा कामः । क्रोधो द्वेषः । कृतिः प्रयत्नः ।

७२ । विहितकर्मजन्यो धर्मः । निषिद्धकर्मज-न्यस्त्वधर्मः ।

७३ । बुद्ध्यादयोऽष्टावात्ममात्रविशेषगुणाः ।

७४ । बुद्धीच्छाप्रयत्ना द्विविधा नित्या अनित्याश्च । नित्या ईश्वरस्य । अनित्या जीवस्य ॥

७५ । संस्कारस्त्रिविधो वेगो भावना स्थितिस्थापकश्चेति । वेगः पृथिव्यादिचतुष्टयमनोवृत्तिः । अनुभवजन्या स्मृतिहेतुर्भावना आत्ममात्रवृत्तिः । अन्यथाकृतस्य पुनस्तदवस्थापादकः स्थितिस्थापकः कटादिपृथिवीवृत्तिः । इति गुणाः ॥

७६ । चलनात्मकं कर्म ।

ऊर्ध्वदेशसंयोगहेतुरुत्क्षेपणम् । अधोदेशसंयोगहेतुरपक्षेपणम् । सन्निकृष्टसंयोगहेतुराकुञ्चनम् । विप्रकृष्टसंयोगहेतुः प्रसारणम् । अन्यत् सर्वं गमनम् । पृथिव्यादिचतुष्टयमनोमात्रवृत्ति ॥

७७ । नित्यमेकमनेकानुगतं सामान्यं द्रव्यगुणकर्मवृत्ति । तद्द्विविधं परापरभेदात् । परं सत्ता । अपरं जातिर्द्रव्यत्वादिः ॥

७८ । नित्यद्रव्यवृत्तयो व्यावर्तका विशेषाः ॥

७९ । नित्यसम्बन्धः समवायः अयुतसिद्ध-

वृत्तिः । ययोर्द्वयोर्मध्ये एकमपराश्रितमेवाव-तिष्ठते तावायुतसिद्धौ अवयवावयविनौ गुणगुणिनौ क्रियाक्रियावन्तौ जातिव्यक्ती विशेषनित्यद्रव्ये चेति ॥

८० । अनादिः सान्तः प्रागभावः उत्पत्तेः पूर्वं कार्यस्य सादिरनन्तः प्रध्वंसः उत्प-त्त्यनन्तरं कार्यस्य । त्रैकालिकसंसर्गावच्छिन्न-प्रतियोगिकोऽत्यन्ताभावः । यथा भूतले घटो नास्तीति । तादात्म्यसम्बन्धावच्छिन्नप्रतियो-गिको ऽन्योन्याभावः । यथा घटः पटो न भव-तीति ॥

८१ । सर्वेषां पदार्थानां यथायथमुक्तेष्वन्त-र्भावात्सप्तैव पदार्था इति सिद्धम् ॥

८२ । कणादन्यायमतयोर्बालव्युत्पत्तिसिद्धये ।
अन्नंभट्टेन विदुषा रचितस्तर्कसंग्रहः ॥

इति श्री तर्कसंग्रहः समाप्तः ॥